Withdrawn

PRESIDENTS

WILLIAM HENRY HARRISON

A MyReportLinks.com Book

David Lillard

MyReportLinks.com Books

an imprint of

Enslow Publishers, Inc.

Box 398, 40 Industrial Road

Berkeley Heights, NJ 07922

USA

Thank you to Glenn Scherer, who contributed substantially and significantly to the research and writing of this book.

MyReportLinks.com Books, an imprint of Enslow Publishers, Inc. MyReportLinks is a trademark of Enslow Publishers, Inc.

Library of Congress Cataloging-in-Publication Data

Lillard, David.
  William Henry Harrison / David Lillard.
     p. cm. — (Presidents)
Summary: Describes the childhood, military and political career, short presidency, untimely death, and legacy of America's ninth president.
Includes Internet links to web sites.
Includes bibliographical references and index.
  ISBN 0-7660-5150-1
  1. Harrison, William Henry, 1773–1841—Juvenile literature. 2. Presidents—United States—Biography—Juvenile literature. [1. Harrison, William Henry, 1773–1841. 2. Presidents.] I. Title. II. Series.
  E392 .L55 2003
  973.5'8'092—dc21

                    2002153558

Printed in the United States of America

10 9 8 7 6 5 4 3 2 1

To Our Readers:
Through the purchase of this book, you and your library gain access to the Report Links that specifically back up this book.
The Publisher will provide access to the Report Links that back up this book and will keep these Report Links up to date on **www.myreportlinks.com** for three years from the book's first publication date.
We have done our best to make sure all Internet addresses in this book were active and appropriate when we went to press. However, the author and the Publisher have no control over, and assume no liability for, the material available on those Internet sites or on other Web sites they may link to.
The usage of the MyReportLinks.com Books Web site is subject to the terms and conditions stated on the Usage Policy Statement on **www.myreportlinks.com**.
A password may be required to access the Report Links that back up this book. The password is found on the bottom of page 4 of this book.
Any comments or suggestions can be sent by e-mail to comments@myreportlinks.com or to the address on the back cover.

Photo Credits: © Corel Corporation, pp. 1 (background), 3; Department of the Interior, p. 37; Governors' Portraits Collection, Indiana Historical Bureau, State of Indiana, p. 1; James River Plantations, p. 15; Library of Congress, pp. 16, 22, 25, 27, 28, 30, 38, 40, 42, 44; MyReportLinks.com Books, p. 4; Ohio History Central, pp. 11, 13, 20, 24; Smithsonian Institution, p. 33; The American President, p. 35.

Cover Photo: The Library of Congress.

Contents

		STOP					
Back	Forward	Stop	Review	Home	Explore	Favorites	History

About MyReportLinks.com Books

MyReportLinks.com Books
Great Books, Great Links, Great for Research!

MyReportLinks.com Books present the information you need to learn about your report subject. In addition, they show you where to go on the Internet for more information. The pre-evaluated Report Links that back up this book are kept up to date on **www.myreportlinks.com**. With the purchase of a MyReportLinks.com Books title, you and your library gain access to the Report Links that specifically back up that book. The Report Links save hours of research time and link to dozens—even hundreds—of Web sites, source documents, and photos related to your report topic.

Please see "To Our Readers" on the Copyright page for important information about this book, the MyReportLinks.com Books Web site, and the Report Links that back up this book.

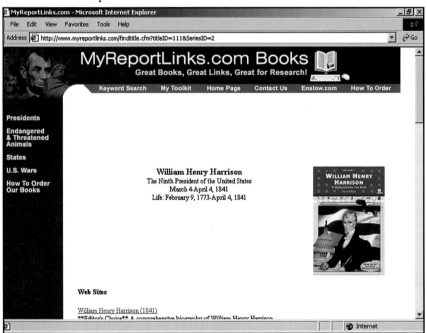

Access:

The Publisher will provide access to the Report Links that back up this book and will try to keep these Report Links up to date on our Web site for three years from the book's first publication date. Please enter **PWH1051** if asked for a password.

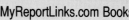
The Internet sites described below can be accessed at
http://www.myreportlinks.com

*EDITOR'S CHOICE

▶ **William Henry Harrison (1841)**
This comprehensive biography of William Henry Harrison discusses
his early years, presidential term, and key events. You will also find the
biographies of the First Lady, cabinet members, and staff and advisors.

Link to this Internet site from http://www.myreportlinks.com

*EDITOR'S CHOICE

▶ **Objects from the Presidency**
By navigating through this site you will find objects related to all the
American presidents, including William H. Harrison. You can also read
a brief biography of Harrison and the era he lived in and learn about
the office of the presidency.

Link to this Internet site from http://www.myreportlinks.com

*EDITOR'S CHOICE

▶ **"I Do Solemnly Swear . . ." William Henry Harrison**
At this Library of Congress Web site you can explore the inauguration
of William Henry Harrison. Here you can read his inaugural address
and a letter written by the Senate Chamber. You will also find
other memorabilia.

Link to this Internet site from http://www.myreportlinks.com

*EDITOR'S CHOICE

▶ **American Presidents: Life Portraits—
William Henry Harrison**
The American Presidents Life Portraits Web site provides quick facts
and figures about William Henry Harrison. You will also find an image
gallery, his inaugural address, and more.

Link to this Internet site from http://www.myreportlinks.com

*EDITOR'S CHOICE

▶ **The American Presidency: William Henry Harrison**
The American Presidency Web site contains an in-depth biography of
William Henry Harrison. Here you will learn about his life, military
career, political career, and presidency. His inaugural address and quick
facts are also included.

Link to this Internet site from http://www.myreportlinks.com

*EDITOR'S CHOICE

▶ **William Henry Harrison: Death by Presidency**
At this PBS Web site you can read a brief essay discussing William
Henry Harrison's inauguration and short presidency. You can also
view a historical document and a video clip.

Link to this Internet site from http://www.myreportlinks.com

Report Links

The Internet sites described below can be accessed at
http://www.myreportlinks.com

▶**The American Presidency: Whig Party**
From the 1830s to the 1850s the Whig Party battled the Democratic Party for
political office. The presidents from the Whig Party include William Henry
Harrison, John Tyler, Zachary Taylor, and Millard Fillmore. You will also learn
about the rise and fall of this party.

Link to this Internet site from http://www.myreportlinks.com

▶**American Treasures of the Library of Congress:
Harrison's Inauguration**
William Henry Harrison was inaugurated on March 4, 1841. Here you will
find a printed invitation and a lithograph of the ceremony. A historical
background is also included.

Link to this Internet site from http://www.myreportlinks.com

▶**America Votes: William Henry Harrison—1840**
America Votes, a Web site from Duke University's Special Collections Library,
holds two images from Harrison's campaign days. Although Harrison did not
grow up in a log cabin, he is often referred to as the "Log Cabin President."

Link to this Internet site from http://www.myreportlinks.com

▶**The Avalon Project at Yale Law School: Inaugural Address of
William Henry Harrison**
William Henry Harrison, who had the shortest presidency in the history of
the United States, had the longest inaugural address in the nation's history.
Here you will find the complete text of this historic speech.

Link to this Internet site from http://www.myreportlinks.com

▶**The Battle of Fallen Timbers**
The United States Army fought the tribes of the Northwest Territory at the
Battle of Fallen Timbers. William Henry Harrison distinguished himself in
this victory. This page contains a brief description of the battle.

Link to this Internet site from http://www.myreportlinks.com

▶**Benjamin Harrison (1889–1893)**
The twenty-third president of the United States was William Henry Harrison's
grandson Benjamin Harrison. Here you will find a comprehensive biography
covering his life and presidency.

Link to this Internet site from http://www.myreportlinks.com

The Internet sites described below can be accessed at
http://www.myreportlinks.com

▶ **Harrison, William Henry**

This site from American National Biography Online tells the story of
President William Henry Harrison. His youth, education, military
career, political career, death, and legacy are all covered here.

Link to this Internet site from http://www.myreportlinks.com

▶ **John Tyler (1841–1845)**

John Tyler was William Henry Harrison's vice president and successor.
Here you will find a comprehensive biography covering his early years
and presidency.

Link to this Internet site from http://www.myreportlinks.com

▶ **National First Ladies Library:**
Harrison, Anna Tuthill Symmes

Anna Tuthill Symmes Harrison never even got a chance to go to the
White House during her husband's short term of office. Here you will
find facts about her life.

Link to this Internet site from http://www.myreportlinks.com

▶ **The Ohio Historical Society: Harrison's Tomb**

William Henry Harrison's tomb and monument is on Mount Nebo in
North Bend, Ohio. A large obelisk rises above his tomb. Here you will
find facts and visitor information.

Link to this Internet site from http://www.myreportlinks.com

▶ **Ohio History Central: Battle of the Thames**

William Henry Harrison led United States troops in the Battle of the
Thames during the War of 1812. The battle marked the end of
Tecumseh's resistance movement and ended with a British surrender.
Here you will find a brief description of the battle.

Link to this Internet site from http://www.myreportlinks.com

▶ **Ohio History Central: Battle of Tippecanoe**

The Battle of Tippecanoe made William Henry Harrison famous and
gave him his nickname, "Old Tippecanoe," which was later used in his
presidential campaign slogan, "Tippecanoe and Tyler Too." Here you
will find the story of this notorious battle.

Link to this Internet site from http://www.myreportlinks.com

 The Internet sites described below can be accessed at
http://www.myreportlinks.com

▶**President William Henry Harrison**
Thinkquest's profile of William Henry Harrison reviews the highlights of his
political life. Here you will find an interesting fact about Harrison, a quote, a
list of important events during his presidency, a list of his cabinet members,
and a brief biography.

Link to this Internet site from http://www.myreportlinks.com

▶**Presidents of the United States: William Henry Harrison**
The POTUS Web site provides facts and figures on William Henry Harrison.
Here you will find election results, cabinet appointments, information about
Harrison's family, and important events in his administration.

Link to this Internet site from http://www.myreportlinks.com

▶**Signers of the Declaration of Independence: Benjamin Harrison**
Here you will find the text of the Declaration of Independence, biographies
of the signers, Jefferson's account, and much more. This page contains the
biography of signer Benjamin Harrison, the father of William Henry Harrison
and great-grandfather of President Benjamin Harrison.

Link to this Internet site from http://www.myreportlinks.com

▶**Tecumseh**
Chief Tecumseh of the Shawnee led one of the most successful American
Indian military campaigns against the United States. He participated in the
battles of Fort Detroit, Michilimackinac, Fort Dearborn, Frenchtown,
Fort Meigs, and Thames River. Here you will find his biography.

Link to this Internet site from http://www.myreportlinks.com

▶**Virginia's James River Plantations: Berkeley**
Berkeley Plantation was the birthplace of Benjamin Harrison and later of his
son, President William Henry Harrison. The plantation was also the site of
the first official American Thanksgiving. Here you will find Berkeley
Plantation history and visitor information.

Link to this Internet site from http://www.myreportlinks.com

▶**War of 1812**
This comprehensive War of 1812 Web site discusses the war, the people
involved, battles that took place, where they took place, and offers images
of the war.

Link to this Internet site from http://www.myreportlinks.com

Report Links

The Internet sites described below can be accessed at
http://www.myreportlinks.com

▶The White House: Anna Tuthill Symmes Harrison
The official White House Web site holds the biography of First Lady
Anna Tuthill Symmes Harrison. Here you will learn about her early life,
her marriage to Harrison, and her years spent after the president's death.

Link to this Internet site from http://www.myreportlinks.com

▶The White House: William Henry Harrison
The official White House Web site holds the biography of William
Henry Harrison. Here you will learn about Harrison's life, election,
and presidency.

Link to this Internet site from http://www.myreportlinks.com

▶William Henry Harrison
"Getting the Message Out! National Political Campaign Materials,
1840–1860" is a Web site that explores politics in antebellum America.
Here you will find the complete text of two of William Henry
Harrison's 1840 campaign biographies.

Link to this Internet site from http://www.myreportlinks.com

▶William Henry Harrison Steals Western Illinois From the Sauk and Fox
This Web site from the Illinois Periodicals Online Project discusses
William Henry Harrison's dealings with American Indians in Western
Illinois during his term as governor of the Indiana Territory.

Link to this Internet site from http://www.myreportlinks.com

▶William Henry Harrison and the West
This site offers a comprehensive account of the Harrison years in the
West. Background information about the region before and during
Harrison's time is also included.

Link to this Internet site from http://www.myreportlinks.com

▶*World Almanac for Kids Online:* William Henry Harrison
The *World Almanac for Kids Online* Web site provides basic facts about
William Henry Harrison and his presidency. In particular, you will
learn about Harrison's military career and the presidential campaign
of 1840.

Link to this Internet site from http://www.myreportlinks.com

 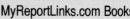

Highlights

1773—*Feb. 9:* Born at Berkeley Plantation, Charles City County, Virginia.

1787–1790—Attends Hampden-Sydney College.

1791—Attends University of Pennsylvania Medical School, College of Physicians and Surgeons, in Philadelphia; leaves college to join the army.

1794—Fights at the Battle of Fallen Timbers.

1795—*Nov. 25:* Marries Anna Symmes.

1798—Is appointed secretary of the Northwest Territory.

1799—Elected first territorial delegate to Congress from the Northwest Territory.

1800—Is appointed governor of Indiana Territory; serves in that position until 1812.

1811—Fights at the Battle of Tippecanoe against the Shawnee; Harrison earns nickname "Old Tippecanoe."

1813—During War of 1812, fights at the Battle of Thames River in Canada, in which Tecumseh is killed; Harrison's fame as war hero is assured.

1816—Elected to United States House of Representatives, representing Ohio.

1819—Elected Ohio state senator.

1825—Elected to United States Senate as senator from Ohio.

1828—Is appointed United States Minister to Colombia by President John Quincy Adams; is recalled by President Andrew Jackson in 1929 and returns to the United States in February 1830.

1830—Retires to his farm in North Bend, Ohio.

1834—Is appointed clerk of the court of common pleas, Hamilton County, Ohio.

1836—Runs unsuccessfully for president; defeated by Martin Van Buren.

1840—Runs again for president; defeats incumbent president Martin Van Buren and becomes the first Whig elected president.

1841—*March 4:* Harrison is inaugurated the ninth U.S. president.

　—*April 4:* Dies of pneumonia at age sixty-eight in Washington, D.C., the first president to die in office.

"Old Tippecanoe"

As governor of the Indiana Territory from 1800 to 1812, William Henry Harrison negotiated treaties with American Indian tribal leaders in the region. Those treaties gave the United States government millions of acres of land and opened up vast areas to white settlement for the first time. But the treaties were not accepted by all Indian groups,

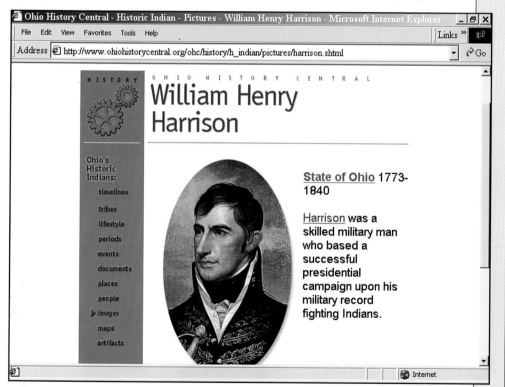

Ohio History Central - Historic Indian - Pictures - William Henry Harrison - Microsoft Internet Explorer

File   Edit   View   Favorites   Tools   Help   Links »

Address   http://www.ohiohistorycentral.org/ohc/history/h_indian/pictures/harrison.shtml   Go

HISTORY   OHIO HISTORY CENTRAL

William Henry Harrison

Ohio's Historic Indians:

timelines
tribes
lifestyle
periods
events
documents
places
people
▶ images
maps
artifacts

State of Ohio 1773-1840

Harrison was a skilled military man who based a successful presidential campaign upon his military record fighting Indians.

Internet

▲ *During William Henry Harrison's military career, he rose in rank from ensign to major general. His service began in 1791 and ended during the War of 1812, but it was his participation in the Indian Wars that earned "Old Tippecanoe" lasting fame.*

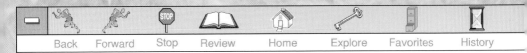

and in particular they were condemned by Tecumseh, a powerful Shawnee, and his brother Tenskwatawa, also known as the Prophet. Tecumseh decided to form a confederacy among the tribes of the region to regain tribal lands and reestablish the Indians' strength. While he was away recruiting more tribes for the confederacy, Indian attacks on white settlements continued in the territory. Harrison, with the federal government's authorization, led a group of 300 regular soldiers and about 650 militia to put an end to the attacks. Harrison and his men were camped along the Tippecanoe Creek, near Prophetstown, the Shawnee confederacy's stronghold.

▶ The Battle of Tippecanoe

Commander William Henry Harrison's troops awoke before dawn on the morning of November 7, 1811, to the sound of gunfire and bullets whistling overhead. It had been Harrison's plan to attack the Prophet and his men that morning, but their warriors had attacked him first.

"I had just time to think that some sentinel was alarmed and had fired his rifle without a real cause, when I heard . . . an awful Indian yell all around the encampment. . . . I saw the Indians charging our line most furiously," remembered soldier Isaac Naylor [1]

The Battle of Tippecanoe had begun. The Indians let go a deadly burst of musket fire that ripped into tents and campfires. They charged and tore through the soldiers' thin battle lines and into the camp, killing some men before they could get out of their tents.

Commander Harrison, looking for his gray horse, could not find it. So he climbed onto a dark-colored mount. An aide jumped on the back of Harrison's gray horse and was immediately knocked dead from the saddle

 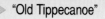
in a rain of bullets. The Indians, knowing the general's horse, thought they had killed Harrison and were victorious. Just before the battle, the Prophet had told his warriors that above all else they must kill the "great war chief of the whites."[2] But that "great war chief," William Henry Harrison, still lived, rallying his men against the attack.

The Indians, who had also been told by the Prophet that the bullets in the soldiers' guns would not harm them and that their enemy would run away, found instead that the soldiers fought hard. "I never saw men fight with more courage than these did after it began to grow light," recalled Shabonee, an Indian who was in the battle.[3]

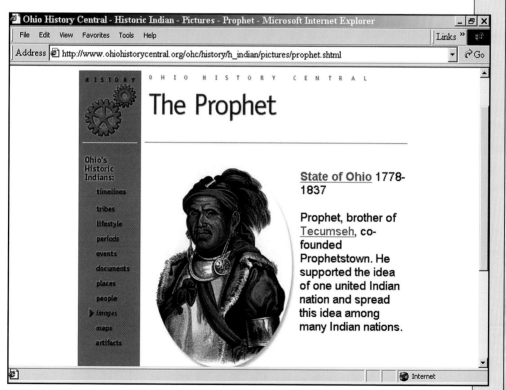

Ohio History Central - Historic Indian - Pictures - Prophet - Microsoft Internet Explorer

File   Edit   View   Favorites   Tools   Help   Links »

Address   http://www.ohiohistorycentral.org/ohc/history/h_indian/pictures/prophet.shtml   Go

HISTORY   O H I O   H I S T O R Y   C E N T R A L

The Prophet

Ohio's
Historic
Indians:

timelines
tribes
lifestyle
periods
events
documents
places
people
▶ images
maps
artifacts

State of Ohio 1778-1837

Prophet, brother of Tecumseh, co-founded Prophetstown. He supported the idea of one united Indian nation and spread this idea among many Indian nations.

Internet

▲ *Tecumseh's brother lacked his physical abilities and hunting skill but he was considered a medicine man and spiritual leader, at least by some. He claimed that a vision before the Battle of Tippecanoe ensured victory for his people.*

Harrison and his men recovered from the surprise attack. They pushed the Indians out of the camp in fierce hand-to-hand combat and back toward their town. "The Indians were driven by the infantry at the point of the bayonet, and the dragoons pursued and forced them into a marsh, where they could not be followed," wrote Harrison in his official battle report.[4]

The Indians, discouraged that the Prophet's predictions of easy victory had not come true, ran away and abandoned their homes in Prophetstown. Harrison's soldiers marched into the empty village and burned it down.

Weeks later, Tecumseh returned to Prophetstown to find only ashes. He was enraged with Harrison for using troops against his people in territory he considered theirs. He was also angry with his brother, the Prophet, for attacking the soldiers before the Shawnee's forces could be strengthened.

▶ A Short Battle, but Lasting Fame

The Battle of Tippecanoe lasted for only two hours. Neither side won a decisive victory. Harrison's troops and the Prophet's men fought to a draw with about 200 men killed and wounded on each side. But the battle had lasting effects. It disheartened the Indians, who had been led to believe by the Prophet that they could easily destroy the army of white soldiers, and led to a breakup in the confederacy.

For American citizens in the eastern United States, news of the Battle of Tippecanoe brought joy. Newspapers inaccurately called it a great victory, helping build the confidence of the young nation. The news also made the name "William Henry Harrison" known to everyone, paving the way for the soldier who had earned the nickname "Old Tippecanoe" to become president.

Chapter 2 ▶

Harrison's Early Years, 1773–1791

William Henry Harrison would one day win the U.S. presidency by claiming he was a man of the people and of the western frontier. His family would have been surprised to hear that claim, however.

Harrison was born into a wealthy, aristocratic southern family. His father was a famous Virginian and one of

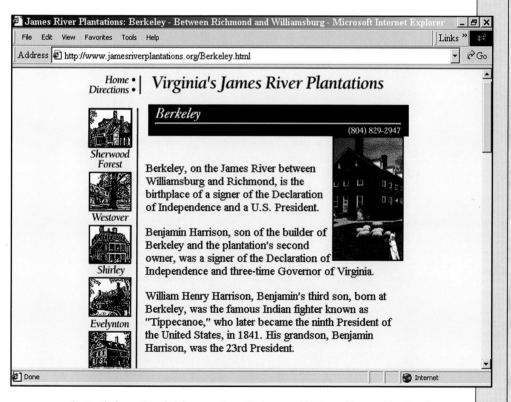

Berkeley, the brick mansion that was William Henry Harrison's birthplace, was built in 1726 on a plantation overlooking the James River and is said to be the oldest house in Virginia that can prove its date.

the signers of the Declaration of Independence. In fact, William Henry Harrison was descended not from the common people, but from British royalty. He could trace his ancestry to England's King Henry III.[1]

▶ Early Life

William Henry Harrison always said that he was a child of the American Revolution. He was born at Berkeley Plantation on the James River, in Charles City County, Virginia, February 9, 1773, just two years before the Revolutionary War battles at Lexington and Concord were fought.

His father, Benjamin Harrison, was a wealthy Virginia politician who had served three terms as colonial governor. His mother, Elizabeth Bassett Harrison, was also from a wealthy Virginia family that had roots in America nearly as old as the colonies. Both parents were close friends of George Washington's family.

▲ Benjamin Harrison, William Henry Harrison's father, was one of the signers of the Declaration of Independence. He is pictured at the far left in this famous painting by John Trumbull.

William Henry was the youngest of seven children. He had four older sisters (Elizabeth, Anna, Lucy, and Sarah), and two older brothers (Benjamin and Carter). Being the youngest had a huge impact on William Henry Harrison throughout his life, because it meant his older siblings would come first in inheriting the family fortune. Without an inheritance, William Henry would have to find a career and support himself.

Another event that may have left its mark on William Henry, leading him to want to become a soldier so that he could protect people, was his first brush with war. During the American Revolution, when he was only eight years old, his family had a narrow escape. They learned that troops loyal to the King of England were going to attack Berkeley Plantation. The Loyalists were seeking revenge against William Henry's father, who had declared his loyalties to those colonists seeking independence from Great Britain. The family fled to safety, but the raiders burned all their furniture, killed the family's livestock, and stole their slaves and horses. Shortly after that, the Harrisons moved to Richmond, Virginia.[2]

Conflict Between Father and Son

Like many young men from rich southern plantation families, William Henry was educated not at school but at home, by tutors. His education focused on the classics— Greek and Latin literature and philosophy.

Because William Henry did not stand to inherit money or property, his father knew that his youngest son needed a profession. The most common careers for young aristocrats of the time were in medicine, law, the church, or the military. For young William Henry, the choice was

clear: become a military officer and experience everything the new country's frontier had to offer.

But Benjamin Harrison decided that his son should become a doctor. He enrolled his fourteen-year-old son at Hampden-Sydney College, in Virginia, to begin studies that would prepare him to become a doctor. William Henry showed little interest in medicine while at college, however. He studied geography, history, and math, but he especially liked military history.

▶ Medical Studies in Philadelphia

In 1791, still living out his father's dream, William Henry Harrison went to Philadelphia to study medicine at the University of Pennsylvania Medical School, College of Physicians and Surgeons. He studied under Dr. Benjamin Rush, a famous physician who, like Harrison's father, was a signer of the Declaration of Independence.

Almost immediately upon his arrival in Philadelphia, the eighteen-year-old Harrison learned that his father had died and that the Harrison estate had gone to his older siblings. Overnight, William Henry Harrison went from being a teenage member of elite society to being a struggling young man of limited money and means. For a time, he pursued his father's wish that he become a doctor, but the money for his education soon ran out.

His reputation as the son of a famous Virginian could still open doors for him, however. Without his father insisting he become a doctor, and with no other way to support himself, William Henry Harrison quit his medical studies. He looked westward and toward the military.

Chapter 3

Soldier to Statesman, 1791–1836

William Henry Harrison was determined to give up the comfortable surroundings of Philadelphia, become a professional soldier, and rough it on the American frontier. He joined the army in 1791. With the help of George Washington, he began his military career as an ensign with the First Infantry Regiment.[1]

One of Harrison's first duties was to recruit eighty "green" men (untrained as soldiers) from Philadelphia and lead them to Fort Pitt, now Pittsburgh, Pennsylvania. This company of men was to be paid just two dollars each per month to march into and defend what was then called the Northwest Territory, a wild part of the country that American Indians and settlers were fighting over. This vast area would one day become the states of Ohio, Indiana, Illinois, Wisconsin, and Michigan.

Harrison and his small company of troops arrived at the height of an Indian war in which 600 soldiers had just been killed. Pushing past Fort Pitt to Fort Washington, they saw terror-stricken men and women who had just run many miles through the forest to escape Indians who were pursuing them.[2]

In 1793, Harrison was promoted to serve under Major General "Mad" Anthony Wayne, who had earned that nickname for his daring exploits during the Revolutionary War. The U.S. Army's mission in the Northwest Territory was to control the region's many Indian tribes, which included the Ottawa, Chippewa, Shawnee, and Potawatomie.

▶ Fallen Timbers

The tribes of the Northwest Territory were defeated by Wayne's forces on August 20, 1794, at the Battle of Fallen Timbers, which took place near what is today Toledo, Ohio. In that battle, Lieutenant Harrison held his fellow soldiers in line and kept them from retreating. For that he received a commendation for his "bravery in exciting the troops to press for victory."[3] In 1795, the Indian wars in the Northwest Territory ended with the signing of the Treaty of Greenville. With that treaty, some of the region's tribal leaders gave up 25,000 acres of land in Ohio to the

Ohio History Central - Historic Indian - Pictures - Battle of Fallen Timbers - Microsoft Internet Explorer

File Edit View Favorites Tools Help   Links »

Address http://www.ohiohistorycentral.org/ohc/history/h_indian/pictures/battimbr.shtml

Battle of Fallen Timbers

Ohio's
Historic
Indians:

timelines
tribes
lifestyle
periods
events
documents
places
people
▶ images
maps
artifacts

Northwest Territory
1794

At the <u>Battle of Fallen Timbers</u> the army of General Anthony Wayne defeated the combined forces of

▲ At the Battle of Fallen Timbers, Harrison served as aide-de-camp to General Anthony Wayne. The United States Army's victory over American Indians in that battle opened much of Ohio to white settlement—and meant most of the Indians were driven out forever.

United States government. Not all the region's American Indians agreed with that treaty, however.

Marriage and Children

That same year, 1795, William Henry Harrison, at age twenty-two, married Anna Tuthill Symmes. She was the daughter of John Symmes, chief justice of New Jersey's supreme court.

Anna Symmes, like William Henry Harrison, was a child of the American Revolution, and also like him, she had had a narrow escape from the British as a child. When her home state of New Jersey was occupied by British troops, Anna's father dressed himself up as a red-coat (a British soldier) and whisked Anna and himself away to safety.

After receiving an education in New York boarding schools, Anna Symmes later went west with her father to that part of the Northwest Territory known as the Ohio Country. He had bought 500,000 acres of land there. In Cincinnati, she met Lieutenant William Henry Harrison.

Anna's father disapproved of the marriage of his daughter to Harrison because he did not want his daughter exposed to the rough frontier soldier's life. On November 25, 1795, while Anna's father was out of town on business, Anna Symmes and William Henry Harrison got married. When Anna's father returned home, he confronted his new son-in-law and demanded to know how Harrison would support his daughter. Harrison responded, "By my sword, sir, and my good right arm."[4]

William Henry and Anna Harrison would have ten children, six boys and four girls. Tragically, six of them died before Harrison became president in 1840. One of their children, however, John Scott Harrison, was to be

Anna Harrison, wife of William Henry Harrison, was a petite woman with enough courage and strength to face the hardships of frontier life.

the father of Benjamin Harrison, the twenty-third president (1889–93). Anna Symmes Harrison remains the only woman to have been the wife of one American president and the grandmother of another.

From the Army to Politics

In 1797, Harrison was promoted to captain, but he left the army in 1798 for a career in politics. He quickly moved his growing family to North Bend, Ohio, where he bought a 160-acre farm for $450.

Harrison worked his way up through the political ranks, using his family name to get ahead. President John Adams appointed him secretary of the Northwest Territory in 1798.

A year later, Harrison was elected the Northwest Territory delegate to the United States House of Representatives. In 1800, when the Northwest Territory was divided into the Indiana and Ohio Territories, Harrison was appointed by President Adams to be the governor of the Indiana Territory, a job he kept until 1812.

As governor of the territory, Harrison was supposed to win the friendship of the Indian tribes and gain their trust, but his primary mission was to protect the settlers—and gain as much Indian land as possible for the United States so that settlement could continue westward.

While Harrison seemed to care about the Indians, giving them vaccines against smallpox and banning the sale of liquor to them, he also arranged the Treaty of Fort Wayne in 1809. That treaty purchased 2.9 million acres of Indian land for the United States and made some tribal leaders angry. Those Indians refused to sign the treaty, and they continued to raid remote communities, killing settlers.

Tecumseh, the Prophet, and the Battle of Tippecanoe

The warring Indians were led by two Shawnee brothers, Tecumseh, a respected chief, and Tenskwatawa, a medicine man also called the Prophet. Tecumseh, who had refused to sign the Treaty of Fort Wayne, tried to form an alliance between the tribes of the Northwest Territory to fight Harrison and the ever-growing white settlements. The notion of land ownership by individuals was foreign to American Indian thought. Tecumseh, like other Indians, believed that all American Indian lands existed for the good of all the Indian people and could not be given away in treaties made without everyone's approval.

In August 1810, Harrison met with Tecumseh several times, but the two leaders failed to come to an agreement. At one meeting, Harrison asked Tecumseh to sit in a circle of chairs with other tribal leaders and negotiate, saying, "It is the wish of the Great Father, the President of the United States, that you do so." Tecumseh responded, "My Father?—The Sun is my father, the Earth is my

Back Forward Stop Review Home Explore Favorites History

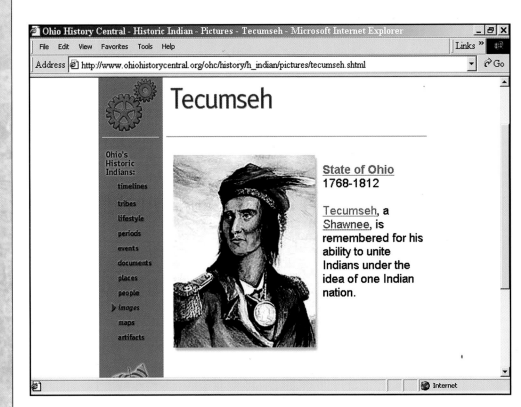

Ohio History Central - Historic Indian - Pictures - Tecumseh - Microsoft Internet Explorer

File   Edit   View   Favorites   Tools   Help

Links »

Address 🔁 http://www.ohiohistorycentral.org/ohc/history/h_indian/pictures/tecumseh.shtml   ▼ ∂ Go

Tecumseh

Ohio's
Historic
Indians:

timelines
tribes
lifestyle
periods
events
documents
places
people
▶ images
maps
artifacts

State of Ohio
1768-1812

Tecumseh, a
Shawnee, is
remembered for his
ability to unite
Indians under the
idea of one Indian
nation.

🌐 Internet

▲ *Tecumseh, born in Ohio in 1768, was considered one of the greatest chiefs of the Shawnee Indians.*

mother—and on her bosom I will recline!" With that, Tecumseh sat down, not in the chair, but on the ground.[5]

The meetings between the two leaders became so tense that, at one gathering, war clubs and tomahawks were raised against Harrison. The Indiana Territory governor pulled out his sword and stood his ground. No blood was shed that day.

▶ The Prophet's Promises Lead to Battle

But the relationship between the Shawnee confederacy and Harrison continued to deteriorate and was made even worse by Tecumseh's brother, the Prophet. He told the members of his tribe that he had special powers that would make the white soldiers' bullets turn into useless dust. He also said that he would cast a spell on those troops to make them sleep through Indian attacks. With such promises, Indian attacks on white settlements continued.

Finally in 1811, Harrison decided to put an end to the attacks. He waited until Tecumseh was away, recruiting Indians from the South for his alliance. Then Harrison led a force of nearly 1,000 men against the Northwest Territory Indians who were already allied with Tecumseh and the Prophet.

It was during this campaign, on November 7, 1811, that Harrison and his forces were attacked just before dawn by the Prophet and his warriors at Tippecanoe Creek. Though the battle was a draw and did not bring an end to the Indian attacks on white settlements in the region, it made Harrison a war hero nonetheless. Ever afterward, William Henry Harrison was called "Old Tippecanoe," a nickname that would years later help earn him the presidency.

William Henry Harrison's ▷ lasting fame—and nickname— came from his battle against the Shawnee at Tippecanoe.

▶ More War and Political Exploits

While the Battle of Tippecanoe had discouraged the Indians united with Tecumseh, it had not defeated them. With the start of the War of 1812, Tecumseh and his warriors fought with the British, who they thought would protect Indian lands by forbidding further settlement. So the now-solidified alliance of British soldiers and American Indians invaded from Canada and attacked and captured the fortress at Detroit.

As this new threat unfolded, William Henry Harrison gave up his position as governor of the Indiana Territory to put on a soldier's uniform again. His rank would change to brigadier general and then major general again before the war's end. The situation looked grim when General Harrison took command. He was put in charge of the army's forces in the Northwest. His mission was to protect the entire frontier, win back Detroit, and invade Canada. Harrison accomplished all three goals.

Bad weather, lack of supplies, and a costly defeat in January 1813 at the Battle of the Raisin River, south of Detroit, delayed Harrison's plan to attack the British at Detroit. Instead, his troops built Fort Meigs near the site of the Battle of Fallen Timbers to defend the frontier.

At Fort Meigs, they withstood a fierce siege launched by Tecumseh and the British. Tecumseh, feeling certain of victory, taunted Harrison: "You hide behind logs and in the earth like a ground hog."[6] But Harrison refused to surrender to his old enemy.

In September the tide turned in Harrison's favor after Oliver Hazard Perry's naval forces defeated the British fleet on Lake Erie. The British abandoned Detroit and crossed into Canada. Then, using Perry's ships, Harrison recaptured Detroit in October 1813. On the short trip, Harrison saw an eagle, a lucky omen that he felt sure meant victory.

Harrison pursued the retreating British and their Indian allies, catching up with them along the Thames River in Ontario, Canada. On October 5, at the Battle of the Thames River, he confronted his old adversary, Tecumseh, for the last time. Tecumseh fought bravely but was killed in the battle. With his death, the Indians' strength in the old Northwest died. The Battle of the Thames also made Harrison a national hero, again.

▶ Harrison Goes to Congress

Although the War of 1812 would continue for another year, Harrison resigned his military commission and went

▲ *The U.S. Capitol building as it looked in 1827, when Harrison was a U.S. senator from Ohio.*

back into politics—as always, looking to be elected to more important positions.

In 1816, he won a seat in the United States House of Representatives as a congressman from the state of Ohio. From 1819 to 1821, he served as an Ohio state senator. Then in 1825, he became a United States senator from Ohio, leaving office in 1828.

During those years in office, Harrison was known less for his achievements than for his ambitions. During his legislative career, he pressed for universal military training for all men, sponsored a relief bill for veterans and war widows, and, though now a northerner, sided with southerners in opposing efforts to limit the spread of slavery to other states.

▷ Diplomat to Colombia

In 1828, Harrison was appointed by President John Quincy Adams as the United States minister to Colombia.

There, he became unpopular with the South American freedom fighter Simón Bolívar, who had helped most of the northern countries in South America attain independence from Spain. That

William Henry Harrison is captured in this lithograph as a larger-than-life romantic figure.

year, however, Bolívar declared himself dictator of the countries that made up Greater Colombia (present-day Colombia, Venezuela, Ecuador, and Panama). Harrison thought that Bolívar should establish a democracy among his people, and even scolded him in a letter, saying that "the strongest of all governments is that which is most free."[7] But the letter only served to anger Bolívar.

Harrison was also unpopular with the newly elected United States president Andrew Jackson, a Democrat. In 1829, President Jackson replaced Harrison and called him home to the United States. But before he could catch a boat home, a revolt against the Colombian government broke out. Harrison was accused by Bolívar of helping the revolutionaries. Although the charge was false, Harrison was afraid that he might be arrested for aiding the revolution, so he quickly fled Colombia.

He returned home to his North Bend, Ohio, farm short of money and deeply in debt. To make ends meet, he took a job in a minor post as a court clerk. To many, it appeared that Harrison's luck had run out, that his career as soldier and politician was over, and that his rising star was waning. But from his farm, Harrison quietly began to consider a position far above that of court clerk—he decided to make a run for the presidency.

Chapter 4

Becoming President, 1836–1840

In 1836, William Henry Harrison made his first run for the presidency, as a Whig. The members of the newly formed Whig Party held many different political beliefs, but they were united in their dislike of President Andrew Jackson, whom they considered a tyrant, and his Democratic policies. In general, though, the Whigs believed that Congress rather than the president should make policy. They supported the continuation of a national bank, and they were in favor of high tariffs, or taxes on imported goods, to protect American manufacturing. The differences in the party's views could be seen in its leaders: Henry Clay, a southerner and an advocate of states' rights, and Daniel Webster, a northerner who favored the interests of the nation as a whole.

In 1836 the Whig Party fielded not just one presidential candidate, but four, from different areas of the country, and William Henry Harrison was one of them. The Whigs ran against Democrat Martin Van

Martin Van Buren, the incumbent president, was William Henry Harrison's opponent in the 1840 presidential campaign.

Buren, the chosen successor of Andrew Jackson. Though Harrison received many votes, especially in the West, he fell short of victory, getting 73 electoral votes to Van Buren's 170. The Whigs turned their attention to the next presidential election and developed a new strategy for winning the White House.

▶ The United States in 1840

Changes in the country and an innovative new presidential campaign plan combined to make the 1840 presidential race between Democrat Martin Van Buren and Whig William Henry Harrison end far differently than the 1836 election had.

In 1840, America was suffering from an economic depression that had begun in 1835 and worsened in 1837, for which President Van Buren was blamed. As the financial troubles deepened, businesses and banks closed their doors. The common people were especially hurt. Thousands were unemployed, and the number of people begging on the street rose. There were riots in New York City, where people protested the high cost of rent, food, and fuel.[1] The economy was so bad that some feared the United States government itself might go bankrupt.

Meanwhile, the country was growing fast. In the twenty years between 1820 and 1840, the population of the United States nearly doubled, from 9,638,000 to 17,069,000. Much of that population growth was happening not in the East, Van Buren's primary source of voters, but in William Henry Harrison's West.[2]

Big changes were also under way in transportation and communication. New canals and roads tied the country's regions together. And by 1840, there were already 3,000 miles of railroad track crisscrossing the country.[3]

Daily newspapers were being published in every town, with editors and reporters looking for exciting news to report to their readers.

Harrison and his supporters looked at all these changes and launched a new kind of presidential campaign, one that still exists today. While name-calling and other forms of mudslinging had been common in earlier presidential elections, the election of 1840 brought something totally new to the political arena.

▶ The Whig Strategy: Cultivating an Image

The Whig Party decided to create a glowing public image for a candidate they felt certain could not lose. Instead of selecting the head of the party, Henry Clay, as their candidate, they instead chose a man known by all the people. That man was William Henry Harrison.

Some people thought that Harrison, at sixty-seven years old, was too old for the job. To counter that idea, the Whigs "sold" Harrison as the hero of Tippecanoe, recalling his first battle against Tecumseh's confederacy, which had taken place nearly thirty years earlier. Even though that battle had not been a great victory, it had made William Henry Harrison famous, and recalling that fame was now seen as a way of defeating the incumbent president, Martin Van Buren.

Harrison had carefully cultivated his image as conquering hero among his friends ever since the battle. And its memory had been kept alive by political allies who called Harrison "Old Tippecanoe" or simply "Old Tip."

So Harrison's campaign championed him as the warrior who would lead the country out of economic hardship and back to prosperity. But that was just the start of the mythmaking.

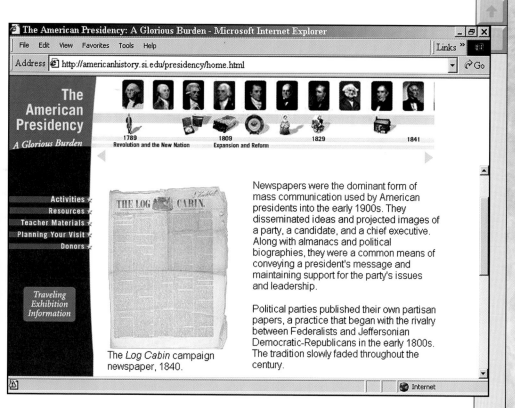

The American Presidency: A Glorious Burden - Microsoft Internet Explorer

File   Edit   View   Favorites   Tools   Help   Links »

Address http://americanhistory.si.edu/presidency/home.html   Go

The American Presidency
A Glorious Burden

1789   1809   1829   1841
Revolution and the New Nation   Expansion and Reform

Activities
Resources
Teacher Materials
Planning Your Visit
Donors

Traveling Exhibition Information

THE LOG CABIN.

Newspapers were the dominant form of mass communication used by American presidents into the early 1900s. They disseminated ideas and projected images of a party, a candidate, and a chief executive. Along with almanacs and political biographies, they were a common means of conveying a president's message and maintaining support for the party's issues and leadership.

Political parties published their own partisan papers, a practice that began with the rivalry between Federalists and Jeffersonian Democratic-Republicans in the early 1800s. The tradition slowly faded throughout the century.

The *Log Cabin* campaign newspaper, 1840.

Internet

The Log Cabin *was the leading campaign newspaper of 1840. It contained pieces on the speeches of the presidential candidates as well as entertaining news.*

The Log Cabin Campaign

To counter Harrison's image as war hero, Martin Van Buren's campaign made fun of Harrison. They said he was so old and ordinary that he should live out his days in a log cabin, sipping hard cider (fermented cider, containing alcohol). With those kinds of comments, they were trying to appeal to wealthy easterners who had determined the outcome of past presidential elections.

Harrison's team seized upon this image and turned it from a negative to a positive. Most Americans lived very simply, especially in those hard times, and especially in the

growing West. Many westerners actually lived in log cabins. And hard cider was then the drink of the common people. Van Buren's people had meant to insult Harrison with the "log cabin" remark, but they gave him a winning image for his campaign. His supporters began referring to him as the "Log Cabin President."

It did not matter that Harrison himself was no common man. Born into wealth, he was the son of a colonial governor and had served in the U.S. Congress. And while it was technically true that his North Bend, Ohio, home had started out as a log cabin, it had long since been expanded into a comfortable sixteen-room manor house.[4] At every point in his life, Harrison had doors opened to him because of his birth and position in society. But in 1840, image proved more powerful than fact in presidential politics, as it often has since then.

▶ Tippecanoe and Tyler Too

After Virginian John Tyler was chosen as Harrison's vice presidential running mate, Harrison's supporters invented a campaign slogan that drew on Harrison's fame as an Indian fighter. Their slogan became "Tippecanoe and Tyler Too," recalling Harrison's military victory nearly thirty years earlier and adding the vice presidential candidate's name for good measure. It was the first time anyone had used a campaign slogan in an American presidential election.

More firsts followed: Massive never-before-seen political rallies were launched around the nation. These events were famous for their rowdy, long-winded speeches, free hard cider, and barbecue. They were meant to whip voters into a patriotic frenzy and to get them to vote for Harrison. Hundreds of songs were written and sung at torchlight rallies, like this one sung to the tune of *Yankee Doodle*:

Come swell the throng and join the song
Make the circle wider
Join the round for Harrison, Log Cabin
    and Hard Cider!
With Harrison our country's won
No treachery can divide her
Thy will be done
With Harrison, Log Cabin and Hard Cider![5]

One election stunt even featured a ten-foot-wide paper ball that was rolled from city to city and through a dozen states. It was a petition endorsing Harrison, and from one town to the next, supporters were asked to sign

William H. Harrison - Microsoft Internet Explorer

File   Edit   View   Favorites   Tools   Help   Links »

Address http://americanpresident.org/kotrain/courses/WHH/WHH_Domestic_Affairs.htm   Go

9th President (1841)   The Series   Presidential History Resources   Election 2000   "The War Room" Game

                                                                    Student Magazine

THE "LOG CABIN" CAMPAIGN PRESIDENT

The Harrison Presidency: Domestic Affairs

Biography
In Brief
Life Before the Presidency
Campaigns and Elections
Domestic Affairs
Foreign Affairs
Death of the President
The First Lady
Family Life
The American Franchise
Impact and Legacy
Supplemental Resources
Issues to Ponder
Reading More
Presidential Moments
In His Own Words
Web Resources
Lesson Plans
Gallery

William Henry Harrison gave the longest inaugural address in history, and it was, in retrospect, a good thing, because it is virtually the only record of his presidential intentions. He had deliberately avoided hard stands on issues during the campaign, earning the nickname "General Mum" from the opposition. But on a freezing, snowing March day in 1841, he outlined his vision for leadership at last.

Harrison presented a painstakingly detailed critique of the Constitution, and how his presidency would tread lightly on what he saw as its flaws. He criticized what he perceived to be a trend towards an excess of power seized by the executive branch, and pledged "under no circumstances will I consent to serve a second term." Past presidential excesses in fiscal management were roundly condemned, a clear swipe at the still-looming shadow of Andrew Jackson. Harrison pledged no presidential interference in the development of financial

WILLIAM HENRY HARRISON

Lithograph of William Henry Harrison, President of the United States, 1841.

Internet

Harrison's "log cabin" campaign capitalized on his fame as an Indian fighter and his life on the frontier. In reality, he was hardly a man of the people, since he had been born into a wealthy family.

it. This first modern presidential campaign also came complete with political buttons and ribbons. Miniature log cabins and cider jugs, symbols identified with Harrison, were given away by the thousands.

Personal Attacks

Also important to the campaign were the attacks on President Van Buren. He was unfairly pictured as the enemy of democracy, a rich New York aristocrat who cared more about expensive French wines than he did about the needs of the people.

One newspaper editor who clearly favored Harrison characterized Van Buren this way: "If you wish to be poor and trodden down and to see your wife starving and your children in ignorance, vote for Martin Van Buren. Vote for Harrison and get $2 a day and roast beef."[6]

Van Buren supporters responded with anger and their own insults. "There is not a man in the nation . . . who does not know that General Harrison is now, and always has been, a weak and imbecile man . . . a man of weak character and feeble intellect."[7]

Still, the efforts of the Democrats failed. The Whig campaign steamrolled over them. Van Buren mistakenly refused to speak up for himself, holding to tradition. But Harrison took to the podium and became the first presidential candidate to make his own speeches directly to the people.

Harrison never focused on his solutions to the country's problems. He only vaguely promised to end the economic depression once he got in office. In fact, Whig Party leaders advised Harrison not to talk about his beliefs or principles, so Harrison rarely voiced an opinion.

▶ A Rally to Remember

One of the largest rallies of the Harrison campaign took place on the site of the Tippecanoe battlefield. That May event attracted 30,000 Harrison supporters who came by stagecoach and ox team, on horseback, and on foot. Old soldiers in uniform pitched tents and cooked up army meals. Festive banners fluttered in the breeze. The smell of barbecue wafted on the air, and hard cider flowed freely.

Grand floats in the shapes of warships, canoes, cider barrels, and of course, log cabins, rolled through the battleground. A twenty-six-gun salute welcomed Old Tippecanoe himself, who stood before thousands of well-wishers and spoke generally about the future of democracy and his future as their president.[8]

When November's election came, Martin Van Buren was defeated. William Henry Harrison, the people's candidate, captured 53 percent of the popular vote.

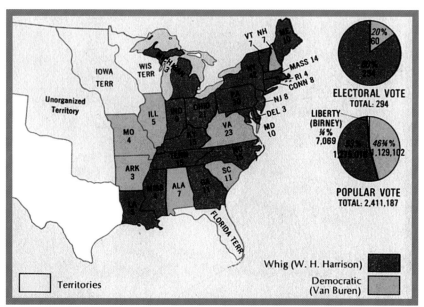

This map shows the states won in the presidential election of 1840.

A One-Month Presidency

The wild celebration that characterized Harrison's election campaign was to be followed by the briefest presidency in history. William Henry Harrison was the oldest president to take office until Ronald Reagan became president at age sixty-nine in 1981. But Harrison seemed determined from the start to prove his youthful energy.

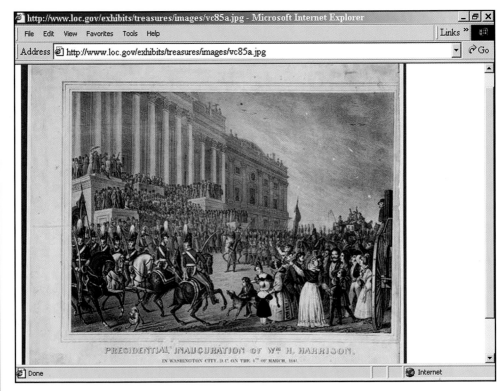

http://www.loc.gov/exhibits/treasures/images/vc85a.jpg - Microsoft Internet Explorer

File   Edit   View   Favorites   Tools   Help   Links »

Address http://www.loc.gov/exhibits/treasures/images/vc85a.jpg   Go

PRESIDENTIAL INAUGURATION OF Wm H. HARRISON,
IN WASHINGTON CITY, D.C. ON THE 4th OF MARCH, 1841.

Done   Internet

▲ *William Henry Harrison's inauguration, March 4, 1841. His inaugural speech, which lasted for more than an hour and a half, remains the longest inaugural address delivered by a U.S. president.*

He rode vigorously into Washington on February 9, his sixty-eighth birthday, on his favorite horse, Old Whitey.

Despite raw winter weather at his March 4, 1841, inauguration, Harrison wore no hat, gloves, or overcoat. And his speech, delivered outdoors in the cold, lasted for an hour and forty minutes—the longest ever given by an incoming president. Harrison caught a cold that day, but rather than resting, he threw himself into his duties.

The *Caroline* Affair

Just a week after taking office, Harrison faced the possibility of war with Great Britain. The reason was a failed Canadian rebellion against the British government that had taken place three years earlier. There had been sympathy in the United States for the democratic movement in Canada. Several American crewmen of the steamboat *Caroline* had taken part in the revolt by carrying supplies and men from the American side of the Niagara River to the Canadian rebels on Navy Island. On December 29, 1837, a small group of men loyal to the British government in Canada had crossed the river, set fire to the *Caroline*, and sent the boat cascading over Niagara Falls. One American seaman was killed in the incident. Later, a Canadian named Alexander McLeod, who had taken part in the attack on the *Caroline*, was arrested in New York after he was overheard bragging about killing the seaman. As soon as Harrison took office, the British government demanded the prisoner's release on threat of war. Harrison apologized to Great Britain and secured the promise of a pardon for McLeod, and that ended the crisis.[1]

▶ Presidential Pressures

Other more serious troubles met Harrison at the White House door. The economic depression of 1837 had left the United States Treasury empty and the nation in debt.[2] The president called a special session of Congress to be held in May to address this difficult problem. Unfortunately, he would not live to oversee that meeting.

While Harrison had been a great military leader and knew how to handle himself on the battlefield, he now found himself defending against a more exhausting enemy: a massed army of office seekers who nagged him day and night at the White House and by mail with

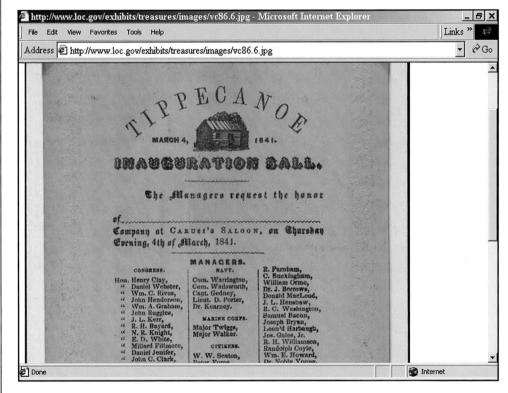

▲ Even the invitation to Harrison's Inauguration Ball, held at Carusi's Saloon in Washington, D.C., referred to "Tippecanoe."

hundreds of letters. These people, often Harrison's friends, were trying to get appointed to positions of power. Their constant requests for help must have been tiring for the sixty-eight-year-old president, who had already been wearied by the challenges of the long campaign trail.

Harrison's Death

To escape the office seekers, Harrison enjoyed simple pleasures like morning walks and horseback riding. He especially liked to get up early and do his own shopping before breakfast. It was on one of these trips in March when he went out walking to buy vegetables that he got caught in a drenching rain and caught a chill.

Within a week, Harrison was so sick that he could not leave his bed. The president realized the seriousness of his situation, saying, "I am ill, very ill, much more so than they think me."[3]

He began drifting in and out of consciousness. President Harrison's last words to his doctor show his dedication to his country: "I wish you to understand the true principles of the government. I wish them carried out. I ask nothing more."[4] What those "true principles" were will never be known.

William Henry Harrison died on April 4, 1841, just one month after taking the oath of office. His body lay in state in the Capitol building and was then accompanied by twenty-six pallbearers and more than ten thousand mourners to a temporary grave in Washington, D.C.

Harrison's wife, Anna, who had been ill, had not made the trip to Washington in winter to see her husband's inauguration. She had expected to join him there in the spring. Instead she arrived in time to take his body back to Ohio, to its final resting place at North Bend.

▶ And Tyler Too . . .

The aftermath of Harrison's death turned out to be a far more significant event in American history than Harrison's short presidency was. It determined how future presidents who died in office would be replaced. Because no American president had died while in office before, it was unclear what duties Vice President John Tyler should have upon Harrison's death because the Constitution was not specific on the matter.

At first, some congressmen wondered if Tyler should become president at all and joked behind his back that he should not be called "president" but instead be called "His Accidency." Some thought Tyler should serve only as "acting president," a title he brushed aside. From the start, he saw himself as the rightful heir to Harrison, no matter that he had not been elected. In fact, he returned unopened any letter he received addressed to "Acting President" Tyler.

◀ *Vice President John Tyler was thrust into the presidency following William Henry Harrison's untimely death.*

Tyler's determination to serve as president after Harrison's death established the peaceful transition of power from president to vice president. That precedent allowed future vice presidents to take office after the sudden deaths of presidents Zachary Taylor (1849–50), Abraham Lincoln (1861–65), James Garfield (1881), William McKinley (1896–1901), Warren G. Harding (1921–23), Franklin Delano Roosevelt (1933–45), and John F. Kennedy (1961–63).

Harrison's death upset the plans of many in the Whig Party, who thought the elderly president would be easy to control. They hoped that Tyler, at age fifty-one the youngest president up to that time, would also be easy to control. But they found the quiet southerner to be a powerful president who could not be bullied by either the Whigs or Congress.

Harrison himself would probably have been proud of one law passed during Tyler's term. Nicknamed the "Log Cabin" bill, it allowed western settlers to claim 160 acres of land before it was offered publicly for sale and then pay just $1.25 per acre for it.[5]

Tyler also took care of William Henry Harrison's widow. He signed into law in 1841 the first pension ever for a president's widow, giving her a total of $25,000. Anna Harrison died in 1864 at age eighty-eight and was buried next to her husband in North Bend.

Strangely enough, President Tyler also nearly died while in office. Tyler had been aboard the USS *Princeton* for a military demonstration. A large cannon called the "Peacemaker" was fired and exploded, killing the secretary of state and the secretary of the Navy. Fortunately, President Tyler was below deck at the time of the explosion and was unhurt.[6]

William Henry Harrison was sixty-eight at the time of his presidency—and his death.

The Legacy of William Henry Harrison

While William Henry Harrison failed in his dream to lead his country for four years as president, he did have a lasting impact on the nation. He created the first modern election campaign, and also, through his death, forced the country to work out the details of the peaceful transfer of power from vice president to president. Although his time as president was the briefest in American history, "Old Tippecanoe" left his mark on America.

Chapter Notes

Chapter 1. "Old Tippecanoe"

1. "Isaac Naylor's Account of the Battle of Tippecanoe," *Lafayette* (Indiana) *Morning Journal,* June 23, 1906, reprinted from *Readings in Indiana History,* Gayle Thornbrough and Dorothy Riker (Indianapolis: Indiana Historical Bureau, 1956), pp. 131–135.

2. Ibid. "Shabonee's Eyewitness View of the Battle of Tippecanoe" excerpted from *Me-Won-i Toe,* by Solon Robinson, 1864.

3. Ibid.

4. Ibid., "William Henry Harrison's Account to the Secretary of War."

Chapter 2. Harrison's Early Years, 1773–1791

1. William A. DeGregorio, *The Complete Book of U.S. Presidents* (New York: Wings Books, 1997), p. 137.

2. Freeman Cleaves, *Old Tippecanoe, William Henry Harrison and His Time* (Newtown, Conn.: American Political Biography Press, 1939), p. 4.

Chapter 3. Soldier to Statesman, 1791–1836

1. Freeman Cleaves, *Old Tippecanoe, William Henry Harrison and His Times* (Newtown, Conn.: American Political Biography Press, 1939), p. 7.

2. Ibid., p. 9.

3. William A. DeGregorio, *The Complete Book of U.S. Presidents* (New York: Wings Books, 1997), p. 141.

4. Ibid., p. 140.

5. Cleaves, p. 73.

6. Ibid., p. 164.

7. William Henry Harrison, Letter to Simón Bolívar, September 27, 1829, as quoted in Kunhardt Productions and Thirteen/WNET in New York, *The American President,* "The 'Log Cabin' Campaign," n.d., <http://www.americanpresident.org/kotrain/courses/WHH/WHH_In_His_Own_Words.htm.> (November 7, 2002).

Chapter 4. Becoming President, 1836–1840

1. Norma Lois Peterson, *The Presidencies of William Henry Harrison & John Tyler* (Lawrence: University Press of Kansas, 1989), pp. 21–22.

2. Ibid., p. 1.

3. Ibid.

4. Frank N. Masgill, *The American Presidents* (Pasadena: Salem Press, 2000), p. 179.

5. "Log Cabin Campaign" *History Wired*, n.d., <http://historywired.si.edu/detail.cfm?ID=381> (August 7, 2002).

6. Freeman Cleaves, *Old Tippecanoe, William Henry Harrison and His Time* (Newtown, Conn.: American Political Biography Press, 1939), p. 326.

7. R. Carlyle Buley, *The Old Northwest: Pioneer Period 1815–1840*, Vol. 2 (Bloomington: Indiana University Press, 1950), p. 248.

8. Ibid., pp. 249–251.

Chapter 5. A One-Month Presidency

1. Freeman Cleaves, *Old Tippecanoe, William Henry Harrison and His Time* (Newtown, Conn.: American Political Biography Press, 1939), p. 340.

2. Ibid., p. 335.

3. Ibid., p. 342.

4. Ibid.

5. "John Tyler," *The White House*, n.d., <http://www.whitehouse.gov/history/presidents/jt10.html> (August 7, 2002).

6. William A. DeGregorio, *The Complete Book of U.S. Presidents* (New York: Wings Books, 1997), p. 151.

Further Reading

Gaines, Ann Graham. *William Henry Harrison, Our Ninth President.* Chanhassen, Minn.: The Child's World, Inc., 2001.

Joseph, Paul. *William H. Harrison.* Edina, Minn.: ABDO Publishing Co., 2000.

Koestler-Grack, Rachel A. *Tecumseh, 1768–1813.* Minnetonka, Minn.: Bridgestone Books, 2003.

Masgill, Frank N. *The American Presidents.* Pasadena: Salem Press, 2000.

O'Connell, Kim A. *John Tyler.* Berkeley Heights, N.J.: Enslow Publishers, Inc., 2002.

Peckham, Howard. *William Henry Harrison: Young Tippecanoe.* Carmel, Ind.: Patria Press, 2001.

Stefoff, Rebecca. *William Henry Harrison: Ninth President of the United States.* Ada, Okla.: Garrett Educational Corporation, 1990.